HOW TO BUILD
an
ENDURING
Marriage
WORKBOOK

KAREN BUDZINSKI

WESTBOW®
PRESS
A DIVISION OF THOMAS NELSON

www.howtobuildanenduringmarriage.com
www.karenbudzinski.com

WestBow Press books may be ordered through booksellers or by contacting:

WestBow Press
A Division of Thomas Nelson & Zondervan
1663 Liberty Drive
Bloomington, IN 47403
www.westbowpress.com
1 (866) 928-1240

ISBN: 978-1-4908-4418-3 (sc)
ISBN: 978-1-4908-4419-0 (e)

Library of Congress Control Number: 2014912398

Printed in the United States of America.

WestBow Press rev. date: 7/22/2014

Contents

Dedication

This workbook, as the book it accompanies,
is dedicated to the crème de la crème
women who for over 32 years have attended
the classes, seminars, retreats, and luncheons
I have hosted to strengthen relationships.

Women who've wanted to learn and grow,
to take their relationships to the next level.

Women willing to step outside their norms,
to take responsibility, to keep on trying,
and to believe that they could be a part of
positive change, healing, and renewal
in their marriage and other relationships.

Women who had the humility to admit
things they did wrong, and the courage
to not take responsibility for others'
wrongs nor let those wrongs change them.

These amazing women have
encouraged me and stood beside me
in the fight to make sure
"happily ever after"
is not only for fairy tales.

Acknowledgements

I would like to thank the many women that have compelled and inspired me over the years to put my heart on paper—first and foremost my Mom, Patricia Girgenti, and most recently Lauren Kay, Kathy Andrews, and Karen Cynowa. My mom has always been an uncompromising example of a woman committed to unmitigated excellence in her life and relationships. Her life and love continues to inspire and challenge those around her. My sister, Laurie Piccolo, is the one with whom I walk through life, our arms linked together. Through every mountaintop and valley, she is there to encourage and strengthen me, with our number one goal in life the same: to hear "Well done, good and faithful servant" (Matthew 25:23 KJV) at the end.

I would also like to thank the self-professed "president of my fan club," my sister Diane Fisher. She encouraged and supported this project before it was ever birthed in my own heart. Her love lifted me, and when she left, she took a piece of my heart. I miss you so much, my sweet little firework. I know we will be together again. Your cheering still echoes in your absence. The story of your life, for those who will listen, accomplishes your vision of being a life coach.

I want to thank my husband and my best friend, Gary Budzinski. It has been a privilege to walk through life with you. You are a man of passion, integrity, and character. Your consistent dedication to the Lord shows in your life of excellence and devotion to your family. Thank you for living an uncompromising life.

I want to acknowledge my adult children and their spouses: Jesse and Amber Budzinski, Gabriel and Hannah Bahlhorn, Michael and Bethany Moon, Brandon and Christa Doto, and Daniel and Elizabeth Budzinski. You make the world a better place and shine so brightly. You have brought to life Psalm 127:4 and Isaiah 8:18. Thank you for continuing to allow me to be an important part of your lives.

Over the past four years, it has been inspiring and life changing for me to be a part of changing the world by teaching pastors and leaders in third world countries with Compassionate Touch (http://www.ctinternational.org). Not only are nations being changed, but each of their team members young and old will never be the same after attending a mission trip with them. I am honored to be associated with a mission organization that is making such an incredible impact.

I especially want to thank my Lord and Savior Jesus Christ. Your Word and Spirit have taught and empowered me how to live and give beyond my own limited understanding. Walking with You and learning to trust Your plans are always for "peace and not evil, to give [me] an expected end" (Jeremiah 29:11 KJV). I know that by living according to Your desires I have allowed You "to do superabundantly, far over and above all that we [dare] ask or think [infinitely beyond our highest prayers, desires, thoughts, hopes, or dreams" with my life (Ephesians 3:20 AMP). Living by Your principles has allowed my days to be as You desired with the blessings of Deuteronomy 28.

"Now to Him Who, by (in consequence of) the [action of His] power that is at work within us, is able to [carry out His purpose and] do superabundantly, far over and above all that we [dare] ask or think [infinitely beyond our highest prayers, desires, thoughts, hopes, or dreams] – to Him be glory in the Church and in Christ Jesus throughout all generations forever and ever. Amen (so be it)" (Ephesians 3:20-21 AMP).

Preface

"And this I pray that your love may abound yet more
and more and extend to its fullest development in
knowledge and all keen insight [that your love may
display itself in greater depth of acquaintance and
mere comprehensive discernment], So that you may surely
learn to sense what is of real value [recognizing the
highest and the best and distinguishing the moral
differences], and that you may be untainted and pure and
unerring and blameless [so that with hearts sincere and
certain and unsullied, you may approach] the day of
Christ [not stumbling nor causing others to stumble]."
Philippians 1:9-10 AMP

What to Expect From this Workbook

When you picked up this workbook, together with the book it refers to, you made an investment and committed to excellence in your relationships. May you be challenged, humbled, and inspired to do and see things differently than you ever have before.

People who have the best relationships are those who realize that it takes extraordinary efforts. Olympic and professional athletes have coaches—not because they don't already know the ins-and-outs of their profession, but because they want to reach their fullest potential. These athletes continue to pursue excellence without slacking.

If you open your heart to some new ways of thinking and dealing with relationship issues, the book, *How to Build an Enduring Marriage*, and this Workbook partner with you, like a coach, in your quest to reach your full potential in your relationships and offers help in the following areas:

- Learning what every man wishes his wife knew about his personal needs, desires, and points of view.
- Becoming more loveable to your husband, inspiring his love and desire towards you.
- Giving up control and allowing your husband the freedom to live his life with no fear that you are his judge and jury.
- Setting your husband free from unreasonable and unrealistic expectations.
- Achieving a better outcome by tweaking and changing yourself so that your husband's perception and perspective is considered.
- Avoiding common obstacles that hinder successful communication.
- Understanding the different roles in marriage and living within them without being obscured by or dominating the relationship.
- Identifying destructive habits that may be eating away at marital happiness.
- Preparing to get through potential problems without damage or injury to your relationship.
- Preventing financial matters from becoming a major hindrance in your marriage.
- Holding onto joy through the ups and downs of life together.
- Achieving true intimacy, love, and friendship with your husband.

- Refusing to take responsibility for abusive behavior by identifying and dealing with insurmountable and destructive issues.

This workbook will help you to individualize and practically apply the information in the book, How to Build an Enduring Marriage. Knowledge is procuring the information, but true wisdom is applying what you learn.

As you apply the information in this Workbook, stretch yourself; think and act outside of your comfort zone. Personalize the principles. Keep notes on the results you see in your relationships as a result of lifting the bar for yourself and for your marriage.

Some of the principles and ideas may seem unfamiliar, but remember, our goal is to make our marriages incredible and out of the ordinary. Be willing to be brutally honest; look deep into your heart; and be open to adjust, tweak, and change. Be patient with yourself as you apply changes to better your relationships. You may slip and forget, but as soon as you realize it, pick yourself back up and keep applying what you have learned.

> "Those who built the wall and those who bore burdens loaded themselves so that everyone worked with one hand and held a weapon with the other hand."
> (Nehemiah 4:17 AMP)

Pick up your trowel in one hand (to build) and your sword (to fight opposition) in the other. We are going to start building and fighting for our relationships.

CHAPTER 1

Who Am I?

Application

1. Make a list of your assets and liabilities. Include character and abilities from the following areas:

- physical strengths/weaknesses
- virtues: as a person, as a wife, as a mother
- work ethics
- social strengths/weaknesses
- homemaking strengths/weaknesses
- emotional strengths/weaknesses
- achievements
- talents and abilities
- attitude

Assets (Strengths)	Liabilities (Weaknesses)

2. Make a list of your husband's assets and liabilities. Include character and abilities from the following areas:

- physical strengths/weaknesses
- virtues: as a person, as a husband, as a father
- work ethics
- social strengths/weaknesses
- leadership strengths/weaknesses
- emotional strengths/weaknesses
- achievements
- talents and abilities
- attitude

Assets (Strengths)	Liabilities (Weaknesses)

When working at your relationship, you are to consider your weaknesses and work on them, using your strengths to do so. The challenge will be to *only* see your husband's assets and strengths and <u>by matter of choice</u>, or "on purpose," refuse to look at his liabilities and weaknesses.

3. Make a list of the things you need in the left hand column.

Things I Need	Ways God Fulfilled My Need

Give the list to God. He alone can meet all your needs according to His riches (Philippians 4:19 KJV). Note when and how He fulfills your needs in the right hand column.

4. Make a list of things your husband needs.

Things My Husband Needs	Ways I Can Help Meet That Need

Give the list to God and pray for your husband's needs. Keep a watchful eye on how you may be able to meet some of those needs, filling in the right hand column when you can.

You may ask, "What about *me,* and what about my husband meeting *my* needs?" You have given *your* list to the Lord, Who promises to meet your needs according to *His* riches. You cannot do that for your husband; he has to do that for himself. However, you *can* pray for your husband and try to meet some of his needs. This book and workbook is about doing the best *you* can do and being the best you can be; not trying to force someone else to be or do things.

5. What are some of the "weeds" you have allowed to drift into your relationship with your husband. What can you do to get rid of those "weeds?"

6. You cannot control whether your husband is loving toward you, but you <u>can</u> control whether you are loveable; you cannot control whether your husband is loveable, but you <u>can</u> control whether you love him! How can you be more loveable? How can you be more loving?

What are some tangible measureable steps you can take to demonstrate these goals to your husband and even to yourself?

7. "Walking through life with you has been a very _____ thing…" What is it now? What would you like it to be?

8. What are some of the ways your husband's life is better because of you? What do you <u>add</u> to your husband's life when you are around? What does he miss when you are not there?

9. What are a few things that are very important to your husband?

10. What does being a "best friend" mean to you? Ask your husband what he values most in a "best friend."

My Idea of a "Best Friend"	My Husband's Ideas of a "Best Friend"

How can you start being a better "best friend" to your husband?

CHAPTER 2

A Woman of Character

Application

Fill in the blanks on what you are currently doing, and how you would like to improve in each area. Get ideas from the How to Build an Enduring Marriage book that this workbook accompanies.

1. Goal: Virtuous Wife

    A virtuous woman contributes to something outside herself and her circle of family and friends.

Currently	Goal for Improvement	Steps to Reach My Goal

A virtuous woman is a hard worker; she is not lazy!

Currently	Goal for Improvement	Steps to Reach My Goal

A virtuous woman is a woman her husband can trust and be proud of.

Currently	Goal for Improvement	Steps to Reach My Goal

Make a list of how you are a *virtuous* wife, and what you want to work on to improve in this area.

Ways I am a Virtuous Wife	Ways I Can Improve

2. Goal: Joyful Wife

A joyful wife takes responsibility for how she looks at things, and looks at the world with character.

Currently	Goal for Improvement	Steps to Reach My Goal

A joyful wife has a grateful spirit; she finds much to be grateful for each day.

Currently	Goal for Improvement	Steps to Reach My Goal

A joyful wife loves righteousness and hates wickedness.

Currently	Goal for Improvement	Steps to Reach My Goal

Make a list of how you are a *joyful* wife, and what you want to work on to improve in this area.

Ways I am a Joyful Wife	Ways I Can Improve

3. Goal: Wise Wife

A wise woman has goals, works toward them, and considers the long-term ramifications of her actions as they relate to those goals.

Currently	Goal for Improvement	Steps to Reach My Goal

Make a list of what you would like said at your 50th anniversary, and what you need to work on to get there.

Things I Would Like Said	What I Can Do to Make it Happen

A wise woman expends discipline and extra effort to achieve extraordinary results in above-average relationships.

Currently	Goal for Improvement	Steps to Reach My Goal

Make a list of how you are a *wise* wife, and what you want to work on to improve in this area.

Ways I am a Wise Wife	Ways I Can Improve

4. Goal: Encouraging Wife

An encouraging woman is mature and knows the power of her words. She does whatever it takes to assume responsibility for her words being constructive and edifying.

Currently	Goal for Improvement	Steps to Reach My Goal

An encouraging woman knows when to SPEAK UP! and when to SHUT UP!

Currently	Goal for Improvement	Steps to Reach My Goal

An encouraging woman knows how to encourage herself and not lean on other people or circumstances for her self worth or inspiration.

Currently	Goal for Improvement	Steps to Reach My Goal

Make a list of how you are an *encouraging* wife, and what you want to work on to improve in this area.

Ways I am a Encouraging Wife	Ways I Can Improve

5. Goal: Contented Wife

A contented wife can say, "It is enough."

Currently	Goal for Improvement	Steps to Reach My Goal

A contented woman frees her husband from being her "everything," and "releases" her husband from being a "prisoner" of her expectations.

Currently	Goal for Improvement	Steps to Reach My Goal

A contented woman is grateful for what she has, and is "reasonable" and "realistic."

Currently	Goal for Improvement	Steps to Reach My Goal

Make a list of how you are a *contented* wife, and what you want to work on to improve in this area.

Ways I am a Contented Wife	Ways I Can Improve

6. Goal: Loving Wife

A loving wife thinks the best of her husband.

Currently	Goal for Improvement	Steps to Reach My Goal

A loving wife is genuinely interested in what her husband is interested in.

Currently	Goal for Improvement	Steps to Reach My Goal

A loving wife makes a place for her husband to "come alive."

Currently	Goal for Improvement	Steps to Reach My Goal

Make a list of how you are a *loving* wife, and what you want to work on to improve in this area.

Ways I am a Loving Wife	Ways I Can Improve

7. Goal: Feminine Wife

A feminine wife adds a feminine touch and warmth to her home.

Currently	Goal for Improvement	Steps to Reach My Goal

A feminine wife *allows* her husband to feel more like a real man.

Currently	Goal for Improvement	Steps to Reach My Goal

A feminine wife expresses herself and communicates in a womanly way.

Currently	Goal for Improvement	Steps to Reach My Goal

Make a list of how you are a *feminine* wife, and what you want to work on to improve in this area.

Ways I am a Feminine Wife	Ways I Can Improve

8. Goal: Healthy Wife

A healthy wife integrates healthy habits into all areas of her life, and encourages her family to do the same.

Currently	Goal for Improvement	Steps to Reach My Goal

A healthy wife makes time and effort to eat healthy foods, helps and encourages her family to eat and get the right amount of rest, and helps her family stay fit.

Currently	Goal for Improvement	Steps to Reach My Goal

A healthy wife doesn't give up on healthy habits, but rolls up her sleeves with fresh ideas and plans for healthy living.

Currently	Goal for Improvement	Steps to Reach My Goal

Make a list of how you are a *healthy* wife, and what you want to work on to improve in this area.

Ways I am a Healthy Wife	Ways I Can Improve

9. Goal: The Ultimate Woman!

Where have you been neglectful, or lacking discipline or character that you need to address to make you the person and wife you aspire to be?

Currently	Goal for Improvement	Steps to Reach My Goal

How can you understand your husband better, encourage him to look and feel good, and be the best he can be?

Currently	Goal for Improvement	Steps to Reach My Goal

10. Read the note "To My Precious Child From Your Heavenly Father." Take a blank sheet of paper and write how you want to live using the instructions in the letter.

CHAPTER 3

Control Freak

Application

1. From the quote by John Adams saying that how the war turns out is in the hands of God, what are some of the behaviors you are working on that will *deserve* success?

2. How are some of the ways you "live worthy" of your role as wife, helper, lifelong partner and soul mate?

3. Are you entering "control freak" territory? Do you see any warning signs in the following areas? Mark what your plan is to take *action* against these behaviors!

   A. You make plans and commitments for your husband before you check with him.

B. You monitor your husband.

C. You speak to your husband in the wrong tone.

D. You need to be in control of every situation.

E. You tell him what to wear and how to handle his personal grooming.

F. Your strong opinions are affecting your relationships.

4. Which actions do you need to *starve,* and which actions do you need to *feed* to get to where you need to be?

Things I Need to *Starve*	Things I Need to *Feed*

5. There are things you must learn to accept in your husband. You may want to write this on a separate piece of paper and throw it away signifying your acceptance. You may want to keep this somewhere where it can remind you that there are a few things you need to accept and check these things off when you gain acceptance and understanding of them.

On the right side, list some of the things you admire in your husband. What are his virtues, his strengths, his character traits, things he does for you or has done in the past: the things you should be focusing on?

Things I Accept	Things I Admire

6. In accepting your husband for who he is, note any of the following areas you need to work on and tangible steps you will take to strengthen these areas of acceptance.

A. Be reasonable and realistic, knowing he has strengths as well as weaknesses.

B. Examine yourself for pride, self-righteousness, and inflated feelings of superiority, and see these harmful character deficits as the sins they are.

C. Purposefully and willfully release your husband from your grip and give him permission to be himself.

D. Give up the roles of being your husband's image consultant, trainer, or 24/7 critique manager.

E. Don't compare your husband to any other person.

F. Refuse to see anything except good in your husband.

G. Learn when to <u>speak up</u> about what you admire in him, and when to <u>shut up</u> when faced with things you don't admire.

7. Think of your husband's attributes and his best side, and tell him some of the ways you appreciate him this week. Ask for his forgiveness if you haven't been appreciative of him, and let him know you are working on being a better wife.

CHAPTER 4

Giving Up Control

Application

1. After going through the list in Chapter 4, what reasons for "why you shouldn't try to change your husband" do you need to particularly work on?

2. What role have you assumed in your relationship with your husband? What role do you desire to have and want to work toward?

3. How can you "get out of the way" for your husband to be free to be the best person he can be? How can you be sure to leave the results to the Lord?

4. What are some of the things you need to change in your own life before you start to work on any one else's problems?

5. Read through the list of actions that extinguish love. Note which activities you need to stop and make a tick mark in the right column when you take recordable steps to reverse those love extinguishing actions.

I Want to Change These Actions That Extinguish Love	Tick Marks for Implementing Action Steps

6. Read through the list of actions that kindle love. Note which activities you need to start doing and make a tick mark in the right column when you take recordable steps to kindle love.

I Want to Implement These Actions That Kindle Love	Tick Marks for Implementing Action Steps

7. What things do you have to settle for in your *own* life that you are just <u>not</u> good at?

8. What things in your husband's life is he just *not* good at that you are now willing to accept?

9. A critical spirit is a bad habit. Refuse to criticize this week: stop criticizing yourself, your husband, and others. Look for good things and rehearse them when you find them. Build up rather than tear down people and relationships. Record the difference in your week when you really pay attention and choose to stop being so critical.

10. How has your marriage taught you how to love? How has it made you a more unselfish, stronger, and wiser woman? What steps would you like to take to go to the next level in learning to love, and being unselfish, stronger, and wiser?

11. The best way to love someone is to allow him to feel safe with you. What are some of the ways that you can demonstrate to your husband that you love him and accept him just the way he is?

12. Record the things you do this week to make your husband more secure with you: not only in who he *is,* but in who he *is not.*

13. How can you be more loveable? Make a plan and stick with it.

14. List some of your weaknesses in character that you would like to practice on until they becomes a real strength. Also list ways you will work on these weaknesses to turn them around.

CHAPTER 5

When Something Has to Give

Application

1. Which situations or discussions with your husband are sensitive or tough to address so you need to "handle with care" more than usual? What actions and steps can you put into place to ensure that you treat these areas more circumspectly?

2. When the timing is right, ask your husband what he thinks your "blind spots" are. What are some steps you can take to improve in these areas?

3. Sometimes your real motive can become cloaked or hidden because of the intensity of a situation. Examine and purify your motives by pre-deciding them here, then remember them the next time things get heated.

4. Read through Psalm 39, and review some of the guidelines found there. Which of the guidelines do you particularly want to work on? Memorize Psalm 39 if you can!

5. Generally, when is the best time for you to communicate with your husband? When is the most convenient time for him to communicate?

6. What do you need to work on so that your words and actions help others become more receptive to your communication?

7. How can you integrate more "solutions based communications" into your communication style?

8. Are you dealing with any "important considerations?" What should you do to address these problems?

9. How does your husband describe you to co-workers and friends? What does he see in you? What is your *goal* for him to see in you? How can you adjust your behavior to show your husband the *you* that you desire to be?

10. Try to make your husband feel welcome home when he comes through the door!

My Present Routine For When My Husband Comes Home	What I Would Like My Routine to Be When My Husband Comes Home

11. Fill in the chart:

My "Ideal" Self (the self I'd like others to see me as)	My "Real" Self (the self I know I really am)	What I Need to Do To Make My "Ideal" Self and My "Real" Self the Same!

12. How do you make your home a "safe place" for your husband?

13. What do you need to implement in your life so the heart of your husband trusts in you and looks at you as his "safe place?"

14. What things do you tangibly *do* to show your husband how important he is to you and that you consider *his* needs above your own?

15. What is your purpose in life? How can the challenges you face in your marriage allow the Lord to change you? How can you demonstrate what love looks like to the world by the way you love your husband?

16. Even if you feel you married the "wrong" person, how can you treat him *right*? How have you been treating the "right" person wrong? Remember, "It is far more important to **be** the right kind of person than it is to marry the right person."

CHAPTER 6

Reasonable and Realistic

Application

1. List a few relationships where you need to raise the bar to see with "eyes of love" more. Make notes of the things you appreciate: the history you have with your husband, his role in your life, his potential, and talents, strengths and gifts he may not even be utilizing yet.

2. What are some of the strongest character traits your husband has?

3. Write down your definition of "success" for your marriage. Write down your definition of "success" for your life.

4. What are some of the priorities in your life? Which things do you put first? Do you truly *live out* your priorities? Which values are temporal and which are eternal?

What I Tend to Put Before My Husband's Needs	My List of Priorities in Order	"T" for temporal; "E" for eternal

5. Which areas in your life do you need to pursue excellence in more than you do now? What steps can you take to do so?

6. What are some of the things your husband does that you are grateful for? List as many things as possible. Remember, be a "miner" and dig deep if you have to! List physical features you admire as well. Be reasonable and realistic.

7. Do you pay more attention to your physical attractiveness than your inner person? What can you tangibly do to develop your inner person with qualities that outlast time?

8. Does your husband feel like he is winning in your eyes? How can you make sure he feels like a winner around you?

9. Purpose to have your husband be a "soaked sponge" and lavish attention, compliments and appreciation on him. How does he react? How does living with this focus every day make *you* feel?

10. What in your husband's life could be a strength that may be "showing itself" as a weakness right now? What are some of the ways you can draw out the strong part of that character quality?

11. What are some of the things that could be "running in the background" in your husband's life and causing irritable behavior? What are some of the things "running in the background" of *your* life that you need to be aware could cause you to be unduly irritable? How can you be a little more graceful considering hidden stresses in your husband's life? How can you put fewer demands on yourself and redirect confrontational issues while other things are causing stress in your life?

12. Life isn't perfect. Like a plane ride, on the way to your destination, you may encounter some unexpected turbulence. You are going to be let down in your relationships. That is when you need to think right thoughts to get you through to your destination without injury! What are some ideas from the lesson or from your own experience that you can employ during the turbulence?

CHAPTER 7

Admiration and Appreciation

Application

1. What are some of the actions you do or words you say to help your husband maintain a positive self-image? What are some of the actions you need to start doing, stop doing, or get better at to raise the bar on helping him have a good feeling about himself, and, consequently, others.

2. List some of the ways you notice that your husband has either a healthy or unhealthy ego.

Indications of A Healthy Ego	Indications of An Unhealthy Ego

3. Are there any areas that cause you to fall short in your love for your husband, any ulterior motives to change him or to make your life easier, or any wrong attitudes that will ultimately hurt your marriage that need to change? How will you purpose to change in these areas?

4. Gradually begin to vocally and specifically let your husband know some ways you admire about him or that you appreciate about him that you have not told him lately. Record your experiences as you say more things out loud!

5. Really *listen* to your husband. If he isn't talking, ask questions about his plans, what he is thinking, or what is important to him. Write down four things you learned about him by listening.

6. Start sowing as many little seeds as possible by looking for even the smallest opportunities you have for doing good. What little deeds were you able to accomplish by utilizing these opportunities?

7. What are some basic provisions you are grateful for?

8. Sincerely make a positive remark about your husband to someone when he is there. What did you say? How did he respond? How did it feel?

9. Be consistently wonderful this week. Every day be in the same good mood. List the benefits of being so consistent that no one has to ever wonder what kind of mood you will be in.

10. Purposefully *think* about your husband each day this week. Reflect on things you appreciate about him, ways you can help him, or discuss some of the things you appreciate about him with a friend or family member. Let him know you were thinking about him with a text, a note, or a phone call. List your accomplishments.

11. Understand how the "WOW Factor" works, and let your husband know when he "wows" you.

12. Look for opportunities to "WOW" your husband. List ways you know would be over the top on his list. Let him know when you go way out of your way just for the purpose of investing in the "WOW Factor."

13. You may find, that your husband's problems have become a convenient scapegoat for your own shortcomings. You can always blame *his* problems for *your* attitudes and responses. What are some of *his* problems that you have blamed for *your* responses?

"His" problem:

My incorrect response:

"His" problem:

My incorrect response:

CHAPTER 8

Choices and Changes

Application

1. Choice Number One: What is number one on your list?

   Goal: To be sure your actions show your children and your husband that your husband comes first.

   How do you show your husband or what will you do to *begin* to do to show your husband he is number one to you?

2. What are some of the things that can tend to take precedence over your husband? What can you do to keep things prioritized correctly or at least help your husband understand that although something may need your attention first it is *not* your first priority?

3. Choice Number Two: Good Attitude or Bad Attitude

    Goal: Sometimes the only thing you can choose is your attitude and whether it's going to be a good or bad one. You need to simply make the *choice* to pick a good one.

    Why *should* you pick a *good* attitude instead of a *bad* one?

4. What steps can you take, words you can say, or visual reminders can you put into place to make sure when you are having a *bad* attitude it will *remind you* of your choice to turn it around? (This answer will be as individual as each person writing it!)

5. Choice Number Three: Accept or Reject

    Goal: To have your husband know that he is accepted by you, and to be free in that acceptance to be himself.

    What are some of the things your husband knows you reject about him?

6. What can you focus on instead of the things listed in number 5 above to let your husband know you accept him without expecting him to be perfect?

7. How can you throw yourself more into your love story to change life from *coping* to *really living?* (How can you make your married life wonderful instead of nothing special?)

8. Choice Number Four: Affirm or Negate

    Goal: To establish and strengthen your relationship instead of nullify and make ineffective.

    What things have you been doing that weaken or negate your marriage relationship that you need to acknowledge instead of making excuses for, and just *STOP!*?

9. What actions are you doing or need to do or what can you creatively find to do to "affirm," "strengthen," or "make firm" your marriage?

10. Choice Number Five: Thermometer or Thermostat?

    Goal: To set the temperature rather than register the temperature!

    What things do you need to remind yourself of and make yourself responsible for in order to effectively refuse to go along with the temperature someone else is setting and to keep yourself on more of an even keel?

11. Choice Number Six: To Add Value or Subtract Value

    Goal: To be sure that if you are around, it's Value Added!

    How do you leave a place better than when you came? What are your unique contributions to people and events, or what would you *like* your contributions to be?

12. How would your Resume read for the description you are *now* as a wife or girlfriend?

13. What do you have to offer? What is your "Value Added Proposition"? In other words, what are some of the strengths people have said they see in you? How can you make those things shine in your home?

14. Choice Number Seven: Look for Good vs. Look for Bad

    Goal: To find the good in others and situations.

Ways I Have Looked for Good	Ways I have Looked for Bad	Steps I am going to take to change the "bads"

15. How are you easier to live *with* and how are you easier to live *without?* If *without*, mark your plan to change that!

Easier to Live With Because...	Easier to Live Without Because...	What I am going to do to change the "withouts"!

16. How would your husband describe you to others who ask what kind of person you are or how would you *like* your husband to describe you to others who ask what kind of wife he has?

17. Choice Number Eight: Choose Joy or Choose Misery

    Goal: To cultivate a life of joy.

    How do you exhibit a good sense of humor and what are some of the things you can do to *enhance* your sense of humor?

18. What are some of the ways you can help your husband to laugh more?

19. What are some of the ways you can encourage yourself in the Lord as King David did?

20. Choice Number Ten: To Work Hard or Hardly Work

    Goal: To know that in order to enjoy the fruit of your labors, you must labor.

    What are some of the ways you have been slacking that you need to work at? List any "weeds" that have drifted into your garden because of neglect, and note a plan to remove them.

21. Choice Number Eleven: To Commit or Disavow

    Goal: To show the diligence of commitment in your life.

    In what ways do you show a cheerful commitment to your husband and your marriage or *need* to show it?

22. What is your goal for your marriage this year and what are you willing to commit to for your part in making that goal become reality?

23. Choice Number Twelve: Selfish or Unselfish

Goal: To live with your husband preferring his needs above your own.

In what ways have you put your husband first and in what ways have you put yourself first? What steps can you take to change that around?

Ways I have Been Selfish	Ways I have Been SelfLESS	What I am going to do to change the selfishness

24. Choice Number Thirteen: Leave Him Out or Let Him In

Goal: To make it easy for your spouse (or any one!) to come "back in" after a problem.

How do you make it easy or need to *start* making it easy for your husband to come "back in" or change his mind after a problem?

CHAPTER 9

Changing is a Work of Heart

Application

W – Walk the Talk.

1. What are you lacking that you need to get before you can give it?

2. Where in your life do you need to start "walking the talk?"

O – Outer vs. Inward Appearance

3. In what areas do you need to start seeing the heart of your husband instead of just looking at his actions or hearing his words?

4. Has your husband been loved enough? Write down several attributes that you can see as part of his potential. Write down several cute little habits and actions he has.

R – Respect and Respectable

5. How can you enhance the respect you show others and your husband this week, regardless of whether you agree with every one of their choices? (Remember being respectful is showing honor, regard, esteem, and deference; it is being considerate.)

6. What are some of the ways you have or desire to earn the trust of your husband and children?

K – Kindness

7. In what ways have you poisoned your husband with your unkind attitude? How can you be more kind to your husband and to others?

8. Do you need to forgive any one? Do you need to ask forgiveness of any one? Get rid of these toxic poisons as soon as you can.

H – Hear what the Heart is Saying Behind the Words

9. What has your husband been saying *behind* his words that you haven't taken time to hear?

E – Evaluate

10. Evaluate your marriage relationship: what are the challenges facing you and your husband as a couple? What actions and strategies can you implement to deal with these problems, issues, or concerns?

A – Action Plan

11. If you're not getting better, you're getting worse. What is your action plan to take you to the next level of "better"?

R – Remember

12. What are some of your favorite or most precious memories with your husband?

T – Time

13. How can you free up more time to be with your spouse, and utilize that time wisely to get closer?

CONSISTENCY

14. What things do you want to do <u>daily</u> and <u>consistently</u> to show others how love looks in your relationship with your husband/spouse?

CHAPTER 10

Rules for Effective Communication

Application

1. What are the major reasons you and your husband don't communicate as well as you could?

2. Are you a good communicator? Write down ways you are a good communicator, ways you can improve, and your action plan for improving.

   A good communicator prays for wisdom:

   A good communicator listens carefully:

A good communicator is mature:

A good communicator knows tone of voice influences message being communicated:

A good communicator asks for clarification if the problem or solution is unclear:

A good communicator knows that communication is not only verbal; it involves actions as well as words:

A good communicator disagrees without getting angry. Review the points and see which ones you need to work on under this topic in the lesson.

A good communicator fuels solutions, not problems:

A good communicator knows what to do when solutions are delayed:

3. Of the three communication busters: explosion, tears, and silence, which do you need to work on, and what is your action plan to do so?

CHAPTER 11

Identity Crisis: Roles in Marriage

Application

1. Studying your spouse and how the differences in your background, personality, and gender affect your approach to life and communication can help you understand and perceive your spouse's actions (and non-actions).

   List some of the ways that you and your husband are different:

2. List the roles in marriage below:

   Man's Role   Woman's Role

3. Why *should* your husband lead?

4. What is the real definition of submission? How has this challenged or changed your ideas of submission?

5. How can you be a better *helper* to your husband?

6. How can you help and encourage your husband to be a better leader in the following ways:

    Be a better follower:

    Don't criticize or undermine his decisions:

    Choose "us" as a couple:

    Respect your husband's position:

Stand together as one:

Voice your opinion:

Watch the way you voice your opinion:

Watch your attitude:

7. If you have been running things your way, let go. Tell your husband that you know he is the God- appointed leader of his family, that you're sorry you've not understood this in the past, and that from now on you'll do everything to honor his position. You will *influence* and not be the *head*. Record his first reaction.

8. If he doesn't want to lead, read him some of this chapter. Tell him, you really want him to be the leader. Let him know that if he will assume the responsibility of leading, you will support his plans and decisions, even though you may not always agree. Record his first reaction.

9. To invite chivalry into your marriage relationship, you must <u>allow</u> your husband to care for and protect you. Do you make him feel needed? Ideas to do so:

10. To respect your husband write some of the action words from Ephesians 5:33 (AMP) on a note card and post them where you can be reminded of what respect looks like: "[that she notices him, regards, him, honors him, prefers him, venerates, and esteems him; and that she defers to him, praises him, and loves and admires him exceedingly]."

11. Note how you let your husband know what troubles you this week, what you worry about, what pressures you face, your hopes and your dreams. Ask him to help you make ways to help some of your aspirations come true. Let him invest in you and his heart will be with you too.

12. Being a homemaker is much more than furnishing and decorating a home and keeping it up. What have you done in your homemaker capacity this week? What time and effort have you given this week to build your home and family? What have you done to make your house a home this week? Have you learned something new about any homemaking skill lately? What you *like* to learn more about?

13. What is your definition of success as a wife? (Extra credit: look up what the Bible says about what it means to be a good wife.)

14. What is your definition of success as a mother? (Extra credit: look up what the Bible says about what it means to be a good mother.)

15. What is your definition of success as a homemaker? (Extra credit: look up what the Bible says about what it means to be a homemaker.)

16. What do you want your life to stand for? (Extra credit: look up what the Bible says about what success means.)

17. Reviewing questions 13-16 above, what things can you tweak and readjust so you can more effectively live out your definition of success?

CHAPTER 12

Set Your Pace

Application

1. Reasonably and realistically, what should you consider a "break" at this point in your life?

2. How can you train your children and order your schedule so you enjoy your normal days more and don't require as many "breaks?"

3. How can you help your husband to be more intimately acquainted with you? How can you allow him in by telling him your deepest feelings, fears and joys – the part of you he can't easily see?

4. Make a "ruling decision" that will trump all your other decisions:

For your husband:

For your husband's role in your family:

For your family:

For yourself:

5. What are some of the things your husband cares about that you need to start caring about?

6. What is your husband going through right now that you need to try to understand and walk with him through?

7. What are some of your husband's needs you can anticipate this week?

8. Send your husband a text or call him to tell him something uplifting during the day, even for just one minute.

9. What can your husband count on you for?

10. Record what you give each day this week of your time, talents, and efforts to your husband.

11. Whether you stay at home or work outside your home:

    (a) How does your choice *support* rather than *undermine* the success of your marriage relationship?

(b) How can you tweak your schedule and expectations so you don't put pressure on your husband to take over when he gets home.

(c) Keeping the end in mind, what adjustments do you need to make to invest into your relationships with your spouse so the empty nest years will be amazing?

12. What have you subconsciously been "waiting for" so you can enjoy your life? How can you enjoy the journey? Make a plan.

What event or situation is a barrier to me enjoying my life to the fullest?	I know the downside; what are any upsides of the stage I'm in?	What are some actions or attitudes I can employ to make this time better?

13. What are the big events coming up that may distract and overwhelm you so that you fail to enjoy the happiest times of your life? What can you do to ensure that you keep your joy and enjoy the entire planning and process on purpose?

14. You can't drive successfully while looking in the rear view mirror. Is there anything you need to leave behind to make today a beautiful day that will be worth remembering?

15. For one week list three things you are grateful for each day:

Day of the Week	#1	#2	#3
Sunday			
Monday			
Tuesday			
Wednesday			
Thursday			
Friday			
Saturday			

16. What are some good reasons to appreciate your husband?

17. What are some good reasons to appreciate who you are?

CHAPTER 13

Problems Ahead

Application

Self Destructive Habits

How can you be sure you are pursuing excellence in your relationship and not being a "perfectionist?"

1. **Perfectionists** reach for impossible goals.

   Pursuers of Excellence enjoy meeting high standards that are within reach.

   Which are you? How can you get better in these areas?

2. **Perfectionists** value themselves by what they do.

   Pursuers of Excellence value themselves by who they are.

   Which are you? How can you get better in these areas?

3. **Perfectionists** get depressed and give up.

    Pursuers of Excellence may experience disappointment, but keep going.

    Which are you? How can you get better in these areas?

4. **Perfectionists** are devastated by failure.

    Pursuers of Excellence learn from failure.

    Which are you? How can you get better in these areas?

5. **Perfectionists** remember mistakes and dwell on them.

    Pursuers of Excellence correct mistakes, then learn from them.

    Which are you? How can you get better in these areas?

6. **Perfectionists** can only live with being number one.

    Pursuers of Excellence are happy with being number two if they know they have tried their hardest.

Which are you? How can you get better in these areas?

7. **Perfectionists** hate criticism.

    Pursuers of Excellence welcome criticism.

    Which are you? How can you get better in these areas?

8. **Perfectionists** have to win to keep high self-esteem.

    Pursuers of Excellence finish second and will still have a good self-image.

    Which are you? How can you get better in these areas?

9. Perfection is being right; Excellence is being willing to be wrong.

    Perfection is fear; Excellence is taking a risk.

    Perfection is anger and frustration; Excellence is powerful.

    Perfection is control; Excellence is spontaneous.

    Perfection is judgment; Excellence is accepting.

    Perfection is taking; Excellence is giving.

Perfection is doubt; Excellence is confidence.

Perfection is pressure; Excellence is natural.

Perfection is the destination. Excellence is the journey.

　　—Anonymous

Which are you? How can you get better in these areas?

10. Smolder or communicate: What are some of your feelings that you have been "pushing under the rug" but may be piling up and may cause problems later? Write down your plan on how to best communicate those items on the list to your husband.

11. Where are you in the five levels of communication listed? How can you grow to go up one level at a time until you are at the first level?

12. How do you need to start making your *ways* known to your husband so he doesn't just see your *acts?* How can you start communicating your *whys* so he knows what ideas are *behind* your actions?

13. How can you reveal your heart more to your husband (one layer at a time if it has been while)? How can you know more about what is important to him?

14. Discuss with your husband some actions that other couples do that you would like to do. Discuss with him some actions that other couples do that you do not choose to do.

15. Understand or demand: How do you greet your husband and what is his routine when he comes home? Why is he excited and glad to get home, and if not, what can you do to encourage him to be?

16. How do you forgo your own needs to prefer your husband's need to unwind?

17. How well do you understand your husband's motives? In what way does understanding his motives help you to deal with situations better?

18. Do you emphasize your husband's positive traits with your children and with others?

    This takes great discipline but the rewards are great. How will you raise the bar in this area?

19. It is important to make time for rest, recreation, and down time. How can you improve in this area?

20. Bomb diffuser or bomb detonator: When you are dealing with potentially explosive and destructive elements in your relationship, what items from the list to you need to work on?

21. If you are angry, what information from "Stop, Look, and Listen" will you incorporate into your life to help you?

22. Have you "prepared for the crash?" Write down several tips you want to use to help fortify your marriage in the section on Effective Problem Solving (numbers 1-12).

23. What are our Rules of War that we have now or that we should put in place?

24. When you feel pressure and are frustrated, which of the tips listed can help you? If you still need ideas, consult with someone who made it through your situation before and ask them for some tips. You may also Google™ some ideas for tips to make it through your unique situations as well. Record any ideas and how you can institute them.

CHAPTER 14

Joy in the Journey

Application

Financial Strength

1. Go over your financial position with your husband and make a plan to get out of debt. How can you live *under* your means until you are debt free?

2. List some of the financial rewards you enjoy or look forward to:

3. List some of the choices being in debt eliminates for you.

4. How can you start budgeting more? What disciplines do you need to strengthen in your life?

5. How can you avoid compulsive purchases? How can you become more practical in your spending habits?

6. What is your Debt to Income Ratio? How can you improve that by becoming more self sufficient?

7. How can you avoid leisure shopping or shopping for a hobby? How can you improve in planning and prioritizing?

8. Be honest: are there any ways that you are insecure in who you are and what you make? How can you develop true humility to work through this hindrance?

9. How can you be more detail oriented and track where your money is going so you can set limits and boundaries? What does your checkbook reveal about your priorities? How do you need to be more patient in financial areas?

The Way You Make Me Feel

10. How do others, specifically your spouse, feel with you? Are you a *safe* place?

11. What things do you really need to work on to make your spouse feel like a million dollars?

12. Is your spouse proud to introduce you? What does your normal countenance show the world: how happy you are, how stressed out you are, how bored you are, or how miserable you are? What things do you really need to work on to become more charismatic?

13. What do others remember about you? What would you *like* them to remember about you? Have you loved those in your life enough? Have you appreciated others, or have you taken people for granted and had even a little attitude of entitlement? When someone goes out of their way for you, do you understand and acknowledge it? Are you grateful? If something is important to those you love, do you make sure it is important to you, if only for that fact alone? List areas you want to work on and how you will work!

Joy in the Journey

14. What is stopping you from being excited and enthusiastic about life? If you want more enthusiasm, make a plan to spend more time "in God." List hindrances to *today* being the time of your life (one of those hindrances cannot be your spouse!).

15. How can you express more gratefulness when your husband or others do something for you, give you a gift, or even just generally?

16. How can you be more refreshing to be around?

17. How can you have a more youthful manner, appearance, and attitude?

18. From the ten reminders to live with joy, list the few you want to start working on and what your plan is to work on those areas.

19. List your day-to-day responsibilities that can be drudgery.

20. List your husband's day-to-day responsibilities that can be drudgery.

21. How can you bring the need for feeling important and noticed more into your marriage? How can you break out from excuses to thrive in this area?

22. How can you bring the need for romance more into your marriage? How can you break out from excuses to thrive in this area?

23. How can you bring the need for sex and intimacy more into your marriage?

   How can you break out from excuses to thrive in this area?

24. How can you bring the need for just plain fun more into your marriage?

   How can you break out from excuses to thrive in this area?

True Intimacy

25. When is the last time you said, "I'm sorry," "Please forgive me," or "I was wrong?"

   See how many times you can weave them into your relationships this week.

26. Put your husband's name in the possessive case with your name after it (for example "Gary's Karen.") What can you do to really identify with your spouse that way?

27. Read the quote about love by Thomas Kempis. How can your love for your husband reflect more of those attributes of love?

28. Do you even know what your husband loves? What would he like to do to be fully alive? Are you aware of his dreams, hopes, hobbies, and desires? What can you do to help him reach his goals? What have you done to hinder him from reaching his goals?

A Love That Lasts

29. Do any of your present decisions adversely affect the future? How can you change them? What can you immediately do to make your situation better?

30. What are some *little things* you can do that will help you achieve *big* goals?

Epilogue

Thank you for going on this journey with me to build better relationships. If you truly challenged yourself to work hard to bring your relationships to the next level, your relationships should be showing the effects of your efforts.

When you find yourself falling into bad habits, or when you are losing steam in your pursuits, go through the book and workbook again. Every time you do, you will find new things to work at.

I know this journey has equipped you with tools to keep building better relationships. Keep your toolbox handy, and your work ethic strong, and your relationships will reflect your efforts!